# RODEO

# RODEO

**KEN ROBBINS**

HENRY HOLT AND COMPANY
NEW YORK

## Acknowledgments

Thanks to Joe Hanna and Rick Scott, who vetted my text for greenhorn errors; Rick Seefeldt and Puck Witmer, of the wonderful Red Gap Rodeo in East Glacier, Montana; the very helpful staff at the Calgary Stampede; the Professional Rodeo Cowboys Association; Lisa at the International Professional Rodeo Association; and "Mad" Max Krantz and all the ropers, wrestlers, riders, wranglers, stockmen, and cowboys who put on the shows.

Henry Holt and Company, Inc.
*Publishers since 1866*
115 West 18th Street
New York, New York 10011

Henry Holt is a registered
trademark of Henry Holt and Company, Inc.

Library of Congress Cataloging-in-Publication Data
Robbins, Ken.
Rodeo / Ken Robbins.
Summary: Photographs and text describe cowboys'
participation in various competitive events at a rodeo.
1. Rodeos—North America—Pictorial works—Juvenile literature.
[1. Rodeos.]   I. Title.
GV1834.56.N7R63   1996   791.8'4'097—dc20       95-49677

ISBN 0-8050-3388-2
First Edition—1996
Printed in the United States of America
on acid-free paper.∞
10   9   8   7   6   5   4   3   2   1

The original black-and-white photographs for this book are hand-colored with water-based dyes.

*For the cowboys and the clowns*

# Cowboy Games

Rodeo has been the great North American sport for a hundred and fifty years and more. It started with vaqueros, the Mexican cowhands, who gave us (from Spanish) the word *rodeo*, which refers to the ring or the fenced-in place where broncos, or wild horses, were trained. The cowboys who rode the great ranges and wide-open spaces and worked on ranches where cattle were raised in Canada, Mexico, and the United States made their work into contests and games. Rodeo was the name they gave them.

The world has changed quite a lot since those days, but there still are cowboys who ride the range, and rodeo is still the name of the game for those competitions and wild exhibitions of old and traditional cowboy skills. And riding and roping are at the top of the bill.

# Rough Stock

Any untamed horse will try to toss a rider off. A cowboy has to learn the knack of staying on the horse's back until it calms down a bit so he can manage to work with it. Some horses never learn to like a rider on their backs. They're the ones who put on the best show as bucking broncs at the rodeo. There are three "rough stock" events, and what they're all about is riding broncs—with a saddle and without—or riding bulls just for the thrill of doing a thing like that without getting killed.

The rodeo cowboy climbs aboard a bronc or bull in a special stall that's called a chute. It's much too small for the beast to kick or buck (hardly at all), but when the cowboy's set, he nods his head and the chute boss opens up the gate and lets 'em rip. For the critter and the cowboy it's quite a trip.

The cowboy needs to keep his seat for a count of eight to qualify, to stay in the game. Then he'll dismount, get out of the way, and wait for the judges to give him a score. Half that score is for the beast and how it bucked (for the cowboy that's a matter of luck), but half the score is for the cowboy's ride—the way he raked his spurs on the animal's side and in general for the style he showed and skill with which that cowboy rode.

He gets eighty points, let's say, or maybe more on a really good day (one hundred is a perfect score). He doesn't always win, but God knows he tries, and once in a while he takes home the prize. The rest of the time the announcer pleads, "Give him a hand, folks, what do you say? That's all this cowboy takes home today. He's got to be movin' on down the road to another town and rodeo."

# Bareback Bronc Riding

A bareback bronc rider, as the name implies, doesn't use a saddle when he rides, just a leather handle called a rigging that he can hang on to with one hand. His other hand may not even touch the horse, which is bucking and twisting the whole time, of course.

After eight wild seconds a horn or a whistle will sound, and the rider is free to try to get down. The cowboy jumps if he thinks he can, or he might get some help from the pickup man—an experienced rider on a well-trained horse, who's there to help the cowboy off.

# Saddle Bronc Riding

A saddle bronc is a little bigger than a bareback bronc, and though not as quick it's just as wild, and of course, the cowboy has a saddle to help him ride. The saddle bronc rider counts on the pickup man too, to help him down when the ride is through, but sometimes if he can't hang on, he gets bucked off, and he just has to hope that the ground is soft. If he winds up in the dust, that'll hurt his pride . . . and often there's something more on the rodeo cowboy that winds up sore.

# Bull Riding

Bull riding is truly the main rodeo event, the most dangerous and sometimes the most violent. The bull can weigh more than fifteen hundred raging pounds, and its only thought is to get the rider down and off his back. The cowboy hangs on for all he's worth to a braided rope around the bull's girth. For eight seconds he's got to stay on board, or else the cowboy gets no score at all. If he does stay on for at least that long, the judges give points for how well he rides and also for the way the bull performs.

News          Photos          Information

Horse News

# Clowns

When the bull rider jumps down or gets thrown off at the end of his ride, he counts on the clowns to save his hide by distracting the bull until he can get up and out of the way. The clowns make it look like child's play, but it's dangerous work that could get them killed if the clowns aren't careful and very skilled.

# Steer Wrestling

Like bulldogs who once fought bulls without a trace of fear, bulldoggers are men who wrestle steers. (Steer is the name that people use for a bull who's been gelded in his youth.) In the bulldogging event a steer takes off running hell-bent from a chute, with two mounted cowboys in hot pursuit.

The first, called the hazer, keeps the steer moving in a nice, straight line. The second cowboy as he comes along side jumps off his horse, grabs the steer's head, and hangs on for dear life. He wrestles that steer until he flips it down, and the clock stops when it hits the ground. As in all rodeo events except rough stock, the cowboy is racing against the clock.

# Calf Roping

At branding time on a cattle ranch the new calves are singled out and given a brand, a distinctive mark, to show whose property they are. That's what each calf is caught and tied up for, and the calf-roping event celebrates that chore.

At the rodeo arena a chute is opened and a calf runs out. Moments later a cowboy on horseback chases it down. The cowboy has a lariat, a coil of rope with a loop at one end, which he twirls as he rides and tosses over the head of the calf (or at least he tries). If he's successful, he stops his horse and ties his end of the rope to the saddle horn.

That brings the calf to a sudden stop. Then the cowboy hops off his horse, runs up to the calf, and flips it over on its back. With a short piece of rope called a piggin' string, he ties three of its legs so it can't get up. The roper who's considered best is the one who does it faster than the rest.

# Team Roping

Team ropers rope a steer instead of a calf, and in this case two cowboys divide the work in half. One cowboy, called the header, ropes the critter's head, then the other one, the heeler, throws a rope around his legs. It's all over when the steer's been caught and can no longer run. A flagman throws a flag down, and that event is done. As usual in timed events the cowboys' scores are figured out by counting how much time they spend getting the steer roped, heel and head.

# Barrel Racing

Barrel racing is the one event at every rodeo where only cowgirls are allowed to have a go. Pure and simple, it's a race against time, a test of riding skill and athletic grace, a show of will and a pretty good measure of how well horse and rider work together. Three big old barrels are set up in a triangular course, and the cowgirl has to ride her horse around each one, careful not to knock it down—slowing at the corners, then picking up speed on the straight part in between—and finally making a flat-out ride back to the start of the course. The time it takes is the rider's score.

*Rodeo is many things: a wild celebration,*
*a crazy stampede, a ride that brings the crowd to its feet.*
*It's rough, bone-jarring, dangerous work—cowboys often*
*risk getting hurt. It's moments of glory and days of pain.*
*It's taking the hard knocks and never complaining.*
*It's the thrill of a contest, the speed of a race;*
*it's courage, cunning, skill, and grace;*
*it's preserving the past and traditional*
*ways. Rodeo is how a*
*cowboy plays.*